The Left's
Little Red Book
on
Forming a New
Green Republic

The Left's
Little Red Book
on
Forming a New
Green Republic

WILLIAM L. KOVACS

LIBERTY HILL PRESS

Liberty Hill Press
2301 Lucien Way #415
Maitland, FL 32751
407.339.4217
www.libertyhillpublishing.com

PB ISBN-13: 978-1-6322-1441-6

Ebook ISBN-13: 978-1-6322-1442-3

Contents

Introduction

Words matter! Words are the primary way we describe our world. Words can persuade, inspire, hurt, or even deceive. In the political world, words such as "red" (referencing socialism and communism, a negative concept to many) and "green" (referencing environmentalism, a positive concept to many), provide the public with insight to the beliefs of the advocate espousing the ideas.

But words can also manipulate thinking and corrupt ideas. George Orwell stated, "Political language…is designed to make lies sound truthful…and to give an appearance of solidity to pure wind." Thus, necessity, many times, requires those seeking power over others to corrupt words so people believe something other than the advocate's true purpose. The simple corruption of two words allows the Left to paint its movement "green" to cover a "red" socialist core.

The title reference to a "Little Red Book" imitates *Quotations from Chairman Mao Zedong,* a book universally referred to as *The Little Red Book.* That book set forth simple quotes as truth, supported not by science or objective evidence but, rather, the guidance of a "self-appointed leader." It was the dogma of Red China, meant to educate the masses on correct political thinking.

The quotes in *The Left's Little Red Book on Forming a New Green Republic* reveal beliefs that are incompatible with free people. Like China under Mao, the Left's dogma promotes "the fantasy of a utopian society," while its actual words espouse hatred for humanity, a desire to destroy competitive markets, and a lust to control people.

While most of us view Mao's ideas in his "Little Red Book" as foolish, we must remember, foolish ideas can spread. Mao's book is the second most read book in the world. Words and ideas matter. We need to understand what the Left is saying to understand where it wants to take the nation.

William L. Kovacs

1

The Playbook: 1930s to Present

*The Left's long-term plan is to radi-*cally change the nation's belief in individualism to one of government control and conformity of the individual. It began in the early twentieth century.

It involves respected institutions, foundations funding prominent universities and scholars, to undermine individual freedom through centralized government controls. Today the Left seeks to use restrictive environmental laws to control industrial production, consumer purchases, what we build and how we live.

"...[A] report was published under its auspices [The American Historical Association] in 1934 which concluded that the day of the individual in the United States had come to an end and that the future would be characterized, inevitably, by some form of collectivism and an increase in the authority of the State."[1]

The Dodd Report to Special Committee of the U.S. House of Rep. 1954

"We reject the idea of private property."[2]

Peter Berle, President, National Audubon Society, 1985-1995

"Nothing less than a change in the political and social system, including revision of the Constitution, is necessary to save the country from destroying the natural environment... Capitalism is the earth's number one enemy."[3]

Barry Commoner, pioneering environmentalist, 1980 Presidential Candidate, Citizens Party

"...[D]ogged opposition can be overcome and political leaders compelled to do the right thing. It is also time to re-examine and change our individual behaviors, including limiting our own reproduction...and drastically diminishing our *per capita* consumption of fossil fuels, meat and other resources."[4]

World Scientists' Warning to Humanity: A Second Notice, November 13, 2017

"Environmentalists, by and large, are very deeply invested in tactics that have worked to their satisfaction over the last thirty years, namely scaring and shaming people... [pushing] that same fear-guilt button over and over again."[5]

Theodore Roszak, founder of Ecopsychology and Cal State - Hayward professor

2

Capitalism Must Go!

Throughout the literature of the Left is a loathing of capitalism. The Left simply ignores the fact that free markets have created our prosperous world and lifted millions out of poverty; they are unable to find any benefits in it. Others want to destroy the system and redistribute the wealth in terms of their own version of "equality" or "social justice." Still, others see capitalism as inherently harmful to the earth and actually want to destroy it and the wealth it creates, plunging us all into poverty and privation, in order to "save the planet." These views frame the connection between socialism and the New Green Republic.

"We must make this an insecure and inhospitable place for capitalists and their projects...We must reclaim the roads and plowed land, halt dam construction, tear down existing dams, free shackled rivers and return to the wilderness tens of millions of acres of presently settled land."[6]

David Foreman, Co-Founder,
Earth First

"We've ended
the dreaded
communism;
we must now
end the dreaded
capitalism."[7]

*Andy Kerr, Executive Director, Oregon
Natural Resources Council, 1994*

"The goal now
is a socialist,
redistributionist
society, which
is nature's
proper steward
and society's
only hope."[8]

*David Brower, Sierra Club former
executive director, founder of Friends
of the Earth*

"Capitalism is a social cancer. It has always been a social cancer. It is the disease of society. It is the malignancy of society."[9]

Murray Bookchin, co-founder of the Institute for Social Ecology and professor emeritus at Ramapo College of New Jersey

3

Truth Is Not Relevant

The Left manipulates the truth to achieve its goals. Statements to this effect are found throughout environmental literature. The only truth to the Left is what the Left states as true, at the time stated. The Left believes that it is easier to lead when there is conformity of thought than when facts and policy must be openly debated. The real strength of conformity to the Left is that it provides a solid basis for rejecting new ideas. Truth is not relevant to anyone whose objective is having the power to indoctrinate and control people whose worth derives from similar beliefs.

"Principles and their truth or falsity seem to have concerned them [the tax-exempt Foundations] very little."[10]

The Dodd Report to Special Committee of the U.S. House of Rep. 1954

"[Scientists should consider stretching the truth] to get some broad-based support, to capture the public's imagination. That...entails... loads of media coverage. So we have to offer up scary scenarios, make simplified, dramatic statements, and make little mention of any doubts we might have. This 'double ethical bind' ...cannot be solved by any formula. Each of us has to decide what the right balance is between being effective and being honest."[11]

Dr. Stephen Schneider, Professor of Biological Sciences at Stanford University, 1981

"The secret to [one of Greenpeace's founders] David McTaggart's success is the secret to Greenpeace's success. It doesn't matter what is true, it only matters what people believe is true ... You are what the media define you to be. [Greenpeace] became a myth, and a myth-generating machine."[12]

Paul Watson, co-founder, Greenpeace, 1991

"No matter if the science of global warming is all phony... climate change provides the greatest opportunity to bring about justice and equality in the world."[13]

Christine Stewart, former Canadian Minister of the Environment, 1998

4

The Depletion of the World's Resources

The Left is emphatic that humans are depleting the resources of the earth. This argument has proven false for centuries, but the Left continues to use it. In a very real sense, resources are limitless. This is because resources are simply the matter and energy found in nature that we humans harness to our use through our reason and science. The Left understands that if people think we're running out of everything, they'll be more passive when controls and privations are imposed, and will submit to domination.

"By the year 2000...there won't be any crude oil."[14]

Kenneth Watt, UC-Davis Professor of Ecology, 1970

"Population will inevitably and completely outstrip whatever small increases in food supplies we make...The death rate will increase until at least 100-200 million people per year will be starving to death during the next ten years."[15]

Paul Ehrlich, Bing Professor of Population Studies at Stanford University, 1970

"All the forests will be gone. Lumber will be so scarce that stone, iron, brick, slag, etc., will be largely used in the construction of houses. As a result, fires will be almost unheard of, and insurance companies will go out of business."[16]

Author John Habberton at World's Columbian Exposition, 1893

"We can project with some accuracy the eventual end of the natural world as we know it. That is, no trees. No wildlife. Climate changes so radical the tropics have migrated to the North Pole."[17]

Jan Beyea, scientist for the National Audubon Society, 1994

5

Humans Must Go to Save the Planet!

The Left hates humans. Many on the Left even see humans as of lesser value than non-human species. This anti-human ideology has been growing in tandem with the shift in the environmental movement from concern about actual pollution that might harm humans—chemicals in rivers, choking air pollution, hazardous waste in backyard dumps—to a concern for the planet separate from the humans who inhabit it. The Left sees humans as pollution.

If empowered, the Left would drastically limit the population of the planet, require permits to produce children and impose draconian living conditions on all humans.

"Building an environmentally sustainable future requires restricting the global economy, dramatically changing human reproductive behavior, and altering values and lifestyles. Doing this quickly requires nothing short of a revolution."[18]

Lester Brown, President of the Worldwatch Institute, 2001

"It's terrible to have to say this. World population must be stabilized and to do that we must eliminate 350,000 people per day. This is so horrible to contemplate that we shouldn't even say it. But the general situation in which we are involved is lamentable."[19]

Jacque Yves-Cousteau, explorer and conservationist, 1991

"My position is simply stated. Within the next half-century, it will be essential for the human species to have fully operational a flexibly designed, broadly equitable and internationally coordinated set of initiatives focused on reducing the then-current world population by at least 80%."[20]

J. Kenneth Small, Professor of Anthropology, Kenyon College, 1995

"The collective needs of non-human species must take precedence over the needs and desires of humans."[21]

Dr. Reed R. Noss, The Wildlands Project, 1994

"If I were reincarnated, I would wish to be returned to earth as a killer virus to lower human population levels."[22]

Prince Phillip, Duke of Edinburgh; President World Wildlife Fund-UK, 1961-1982; President World Wildlife Fund International, 1981-1996

6

We Still Have
12 More
Years to Repent

Preachers of environmental doom have been around centuries and mostly wrong. That doesn't stop them. When one prediction is remarkably off, they just trot out the next pronouncement with no embarrassment. The public quickly forgets failed predictions as the next soon-to-be-proven-wrong prediction is screamed by the Green-dominated media. Notwithstanding wars, famine, natural disasters and plagues, humans are still here. They are still inventing; still offering kindness, hope and new ideas. Yet the Left tells us the world will end in 12 years.

"Not to be dramatic, but literally the future of the world depends on us right now.

This is the final chance. The scientists are unanimous on this. We have no more than 12 years to take incredibly bold action on this [climate change] crisis."[23]

Robert Francis ("Beto") O'Rouke, candidate for 2020 Democrat Party presidential nomination

"The world as we know it will likely be ruined by the year 2000."[24]

Ad for The Environmental Fund, signed by 39 academics and industry leaders, 1975

"This cooling [the great fear before it was replaced by global warming] has already killed hundreds of thousands of people. If it continues and no strong action is taken, it will cause world famine, world chaos and world war, and this could all come about before the end of the year 2000."[25]

Lowell Ponte, "The Cooling", 1976

"I'm one of those scientists who, try as we will, hope as we do, that something in our view of things is wrong, still find it difficult to see how the human race will get itself much past the year 2000."[26]

George Wald, Nobel Laureate and Harvard Professor of Biology, 1975

7

The New Green Republic

The Green New Deal is the latest manifestation of the marriage of the Green agenda and socialism. It is promoted by Rep. Alexandra Ocasio-Cortez (D-NY) and supported by the Democratic presidential candidates. It allegedly would bring about a utopia without pollution, farm animals that emit gas, automobiles and trucks, fossil fuels, and chemicals. It would be a place filled with sidewalks, bicycle paths, trails, and pastures that are lightly used since there would be a limit on the population. This "New Green Republic" would be a perfectly designed political state with a well-functioning regulatory machine that ensures the "correct-thought" by its citizens.

"This is going to be the New Deal, the Great Society, the moon shot, the civil-rights movement of our generation. ... We don't have time to sit on our hands as our planet burns. For young people, climate change is bigger than election or re-election. It's life or death."[27]

Rep. Alexandria Ocasio-Cortez (D-NY),
December 3, 2018

"The interesting thing about the Green New Deal is it wasn't originally a climate thing at all…. Do you guys think of it as a climate thing? Because we really think of it as a how-do-you-change-the-entire-economy thing."[28]

Saikat Chakrabarti, former chief of staff to Rep. Alexandria Ocasio-Cortez, July 2019.

"This is the first time in the history of mankind that we are setting ourselves the task of intentionally, within a defined period of time, to change the economic development model [capitalism] that has been reigning for at least 150 years, since the Industrial Revolution... [China is] "doing it right..."[29]

Christina Figueres, Executive Secretary, U.N. Framework Convention on Climate Change, 2015

[The Green New Deal is an] "opportunity to uproot historical injustices and inequities to advance social, racial and economic justice."[30]

Sen. Bernie Sanders (I-VT), Democratic presidential candidate, 2019

"By the way, I want you to know, I'm the guy that did all this stuff [started the climate change effort]—read RealClearPolitics, it will tell you about how I started this whole thing back in '87 with climate change."[31]

Joe Biden, former U.S. vice president, 2020 Democratic presidential nominee

THE QUOTATIONS END BUT THE LONG CONFLICT BETWEEN THE LEFT AND FREEDOM CONTINUES!

Endnotes

1   *The Report of Norman Dodd, Director of
    Research of the Special Committee of the
    House of Representatives to Investigate
    Tax Exempt Foundations for the six-month
    period November 1, 1953 to April 20, 1954*,
    page 10, http://brynmawrcollections.
    org/traces/archive/files/552952f585af5e-
    f916a246c55fcb7a76.pdf ; Referencing
    *American Historical Association,
    Investigation of the Social Studies in the
    Schools, Conclusion*, (New York: Charles
    Scribner's Sons, 1934), pp. 1, 16, 18
    passim; http://deliberatedumbingdown.
    com/ddd/wp-content/uploads/2003/10/
    Report_Commission_Social_Studies-
    Krey-Counts-Kimmel-Kelley-1934.pdf

2   http://www.agenda21course.com/
    their-plans-for-us-in-their-own-words/
    Quoted extensively throughout litera-
    ture on subject.

3   Barry Commoner quoted in
    "Environmentalism: Cult of Death," Ray

Harvey. Also quoted elsewhere. http://rayharvey.org/index.php/2010/02/environmentalism-cult-of-death/

4   "World Scientists' Warning to Humanity: A Second Notice," *BioScience*, Volume 67, Issue 12, December 2017, page 1026, https://doi.org/10.1093/biosci/bix125.

5   https://www.goodreads.com/author/quotes/12866.Theodore_Roszak

6   David Foreman, quoted in AZ Quotes. https://www.azquotes.com/quote/595240 Also cited in Grant R. Jeffrey, *The Global-Warming Deception: How a Secret Elite Plans to Bankrupt America*, (Waterbrrok: February 8, 2011), p. 155.

7   Andy Kerr, "ONRC's executive director outlines 100-year plan for state," 1994. http://www.andykerr.net/100-year-plan-op-ed/

8   David Brower quoted in "Discover the Networks." https://www.dis-coverthenetworks.org/individuals/david-brower/

9   https://www.inspiringquotes.us/author/9623-murray-bookchin/about-capitalism#, https://www.azquotes.com/author/21917-Murray_Bookchin/tag/capitalism

10 The Dodd Report, *supra*, note 1.

11 Dr. Stephen Schneider, *American Physical Society News Online*, August/September 1996, reiterating comments he made in J. Schell, *Discover Magazine*, 1989, pp. 45-48 https://www.aps.org/publications/apsnews/199608/upload/aug96.pdf

12 Judi McLeod, "The terrorist and the mule," *Canada Free Press*, April 9-30, 2001, quoting Paul Watson,

co-founder of Greenpeace, to *Forbes Magazine*, 1991. https://canadafreepress.com/2001/0002a3.htm.

13   Christina Stuart quoted in Dr. Ileana Johnson Paugh, "Social Engineering of the Globe with Sustainable Development Goals," *Canada Free Press*, July 21, 2016, https://canada-freepress.com/article/social-engineering-of-the-globe-with-sustainable-development-goals

14   Kenneth Watt at the first Earth Day, 1970, quoted in Kira Davis, "18 Environmental Doomsday Predictions from 1970 That Turned Out To Be Hilariously Wrong," April 24, 2017, https://www.redstate.com/kiradavis/2017/04/24/18-environmental-doomsday-predictions-1970-turned-hilariously-wrong/

15 Paul Ehrlich, *Mademoiselle,* April
    1970 issue. https://books.google.
    com/books?id=lo-qDwAAQBAJ&p-
    g=PA145&lpg=PA145&dq=ehrli-
    ch+quote+in+Mademoiselle,+%22&-
    source=bl&ots=wBkZC5GFd_&sig=AC-
    fU3U2PtB1R2skiVO9KcXpgcBY-
    17fJUgQ&hl=en&sa=X&ved=2a-
    hUKEwj8s_r2hvXpAhVWTDABHSqA-
    dgQ6AEwEHoECAgQAQ#v=onep-
    age&q=ehrlich%20quote%20in%20
    Mademoiselle%2C%20%22&f=false

16 John Habberton, 1893 World's
    Columbian Exposition, predicting
    the state of the world in 1993, in "Of
    Women, Literature, Temperance,
    Marriage, Etc.," written for the
    American Press Association for the
    1893 World's Columbian Exposition in
    Chicago, http://www.learner.org/work-
    shops/primarysources/corporations/
    docs/habberton.html

17 Jan Beyea in a fundraising letter for
    the Audubon Society, 1994, http://
    thesouthernblog.com/2017/02/cli-
    mate-change-humans-will-face-pres-
    sure-to-save-the-earth-and-humanity/,
    cited in Michael Sanera and Jane Shaw,
    *Facts Not Fear: Teaching Children about
    the Environment* (Canadian Edition),
    (Vancouver: The Fraser Institute, 1999),
    Chapter 3, adapted for Canadian audi-
    ences by Liv Fredrickson and Laura
    Jones. https://www.lindenwood.edu/
    files/resources/shawdocs.pdf

18 Lester Brown, cited in Dixy Lee Ray,
    Environmental Overkill, 1993, p. 202.
    https://townhall.com/columnists/paul-
    driessen/2017/02/05/the-hidden-agen-
    das-of-sustainability-claptrap-n228160;
    https://www.thepostemail.
    com/2017/02/05/the-hidden-agen-
    das-of-sustainability-illusions/

19 Jacque Yves-Cousteau Interview by
    Bahgat Elnadi and Adel Rifaat, The
    UNESCO Courier, November 1991, p.
    13. https://joseywales1965.files.word-
    press.com/2014/06/0003_jacques_cou-
    teau.pdf

20 J. Kenneth Small, "Confronting the 21st
    Century's Hidden Crisis: Reducing
    Human Numbers by 80%," *Negative
    Population Growth, The NPG Forum*,
    August 1995, p. 1, https://npg.org/
    wp-content/uploads/2013/09/
    Confronting21stCentury
    HIddenCrisis019.pdf

21 21. Reed Noss, "The Wildlands
    Project: Lands Conservation Strategy,"
    Environmental Policy and Biodiversity, R.
    Edward Grumbine, ed., (Washington,
    D.C.: Island Press, 1994). Cited in
    Brian Phillips, *The Innovator Versus
    the Collective*, (Houston, Texas: BEP
    Enterprises, Inc., 2016). https:/ books.

google.com/books?id=CmvCDA
AAQBAJ&pg=PA186&lpg=PA186&
dq=Reed+Noss+Collective+needs+of+
non-human+species&source=bl&ots=M
LnAFm5C8V&sig=ACfU3U3b7GL4llcvl
rImO82p
7ECXRjRN6g&hl=en&sa=X&ved
=2ahUKEwiGmrzM4pTkAhViIjQIHVI
gBWIQ6AEwAXoECAkQAQ#v=one
page&q=Reed%20Noss%20Collective
%20needs%20of%20non-human%20
species&f=false

22 https://books.google.com/
books?id=fBWe9-A9mjkC&p-
g=RA2-PA116&lpg=RA2-PA116&d-
q=prince+philip,+World+wildlife+-
fund,+quote,+if+I+were+reincarnat-
ed,+I+would+wish&source=bl&ots-
=Qv-LRiSmdB&sig=
ACfU3U0jIWTZjHBOpLkS
gBSZLhwaXKXBoQ&hl=en&sa=X-
&ved=2ahUKEwiet4_Hi_
XpAhXGSjABHf3CDdMQ6AEw

BXoECAgQAQ#v=onepage&q=prince
%20philip%2C%20World%20wildlife
%20fund%2C%20quote%2C%20if%20
I%20were%20reincarnated%2C%20I
%20would%20wish&f=false

23 .https://www.realclearpolitics.com/
video/2019/03/14/beto_orourke_on_
green_new_deal_literally_the_future_
of_the_world_depends_on_us.html

24 1975 advertisement for The
Environmental Fund, signed by 39 academics and industry leaders including
authors Isaac Asimov, Malcolm
Crowley, and Robert Elegant; professor
Zbigniew Brzezinski; former Librarian
of Congress/poet Archibald MacLeish;
Nobel Laureate Albert Szent-Gyorgyi
(1937 in Physiology); U.A.W. President
Leonard Woodcock, *The Wall Street
Journal*, October 30, 1975, http://petes-
place-peter.blogspot.com/2008/05/
many-consensus-environmental.html

25 Lowell Ponte, *The Cooling*, 1976, quoted
in Bruce Schlink, "Americans Held
Hostage by the Environmentalist
Movement," Pittsburgh: RedDog
Books, p. 369, https://books.google.
com/books?id=7mkXBaIFpuAC&p-
g=PA369&lpg=PA369&dq=Low-
ell+Ponte,+%E2%80%9CThe+Cool-
ing%E2%80%9D,+1976+killed+hun-
dreds+of+thou-
sands&source=bl&ots=XaUC8Oby-
Di&sig=ACfU3U2SI8Lkpg79cxVCGEH-
efOQbMFPow&hl=en&sa=X&v
ed=2ahUKEwiu4oa7iJjkAhXtUt-
8KHcwMDFgQ6AEwBXoECAY
QAQ#v=onepage&q=Lowell%20
Ponte%2C%20%E2%80%9CThe%-
20Cooling%E2%80%9D%2C%20
1976%20killed%20hundreds%20of%20
thousands&f=false

26 Quoted in Richard G. Kyle, *Apocalyptic
Fever: End-Time Prophecies in Modern
America*, (Eugene, Oregon: Wipf &

Stock Pub, 2012), p. 267, referencing George Wald, "There Isn't Much Time," *The Progressive*, December 1975, p, 22, https://books.google.com/books?id=p-1dJAwAAQBAJ&pg=PA267&lp-g=PA267&dq=George+Wald+The+Pro-gressive,+December+1975&-source=bl&ots=vTJ28AvEW7&sig=AC-fU3U0bzy_49m0n5ydC9dPh-20G8Xz4Skw&hl=en&sa=X&ved=2a-hUKEwjLlvCC6rTkAhWI1FkKHQX-vC-AQ6AEwAXoECAkQAQ#v=one-page&q=George%20Wald%20The%20Progressive%2C%20December%201975&f=falsehttps://www.nature.com/articles/40251

27 Alexandria Ocasio-Cortez, Remarks at "The Crisis of Climate Change" panel, December 3, 2018, https://www.you-tube.com/watch?v=w0IgDgyHEfc, and "17 Insightful Quotes About the Green New Deal," everblue, updated May 30, 2019, https://www.everbluetraining.

com/blog/17-insightful-quotes-about-green-new-deal

28 Quoted in David Montgomery, "AOC's Chief of Change Saikat Chakrabarti isn't just running her office. He's guiding a movement," *The Washington Post Magazine*, July 10, 2019. https://www.washingtonpost.com/news/magazine/wp/2019/07/10/feature/how-saikat-chakrabarti-became-aocs-chief-of-change/?utm_term=.66036c1196be

29 https://www.cnsnews.com/news/article/barbara-hollingsworth/un-s-top-climate-official-goal-intention-ally-transform-economic-0

30 Quoted in "Bernie Sanders' $16 trillion climate plan builds on the Green New Deal," Associated Press, August 22, 2019, https://www.marketwatch.com/story/

bernie-sanders-16-trillion-climate-plan-builds-on-the-green-new-deal-2019-08-22

31 Quoted in Valerie Richardson, "Joe Biden claims he 'started this whole thing' on climate change," *The Washington Times,* May 20, 2019, https://www.washingtontimes.com/news/2019/may/20/joe-biden-claims-he-started-whole-thing-climate-ch/